1968 - 2018

Federation of

CHILDREN'S BOOK GROUPS

Thank you to
our Founder, the Honorary Presidents,
all members of the Federation both past and present,
publishers, sponsors, authors, illustrators,
poets, storytellers and most importantly, children.

And, of course, thanks to all the long-suffering partners
who, over the years, have put up with piles of books,
display boards, banners, newsletters, book lists...

Any errors are the sole responsibility of the History Working Party.

Thank you to our sponsor, the Ragdoll Foundation,
our Founder, Anne Wood and Ragdoll Trustee Carole Thomson
for their support in producing this book.

www.fcbg.org.uk

Telephone: 0300 102 1559
Registered charity no. 268289

1968 - 2018

Federation of

CHILDREN'S BOOK GROUPS

Bringing children and books together

BREWIN BOOKS

First published by
Brewin Books Ltd, 56 Alcester Road,
Studley, Warwickshire B80 7LG in 2018
www.brewinbooks.com

ISBN: 978-1-85858-585-7

A Cataloguing in Publication Record
for this title is available from the British Library.

Typeset in Proxima Nova
Printed in Great Britain
by Bell & Bain Ltd.

Contents

Acknowledgements

The History Working Party would like to thank everyone who contributed to this history. We have not been able to include everyone's contributions in this book, but we will be placing them in the archive. Any omissions and inaccuracies are ours.

The Federation wishes to thank Anne Wood, the Honorary Presidents, the children's book groups past and present, members, authors, illustrators and publishers for their kind permission to include their photographs and other copyright materials.

Every effort has been made to trace the holders of copyright materials in the book. If any query should arise it should be addressed to the Federation at info@fcbg.org.uk

Summary of our Achievements 1968-2018

The Children's Book Award: the only national award for children's books that is voted for entirely by the children themselves. The award involves over 250 schools reaching a potential 130,000 children. 150,000 votes are cast each year, over 1,100 books read, over 100 publishing imprints involved and over 12,000 books are donated to charities.

National Share-A-Story Month: held during May every year with a changing theme and focus. Book groups, schools, libraries, families and individuals join in creating their own activities, competitions and events which are aimed at youngsters of all ages. NSSM has taken on a life of its own and its reach has become far wider than the Federation.

National Non-Fiction November: the opportunity to celebrate non-fiction. Started in 2010 it has grown from just one day to a whole month of activities and author events, in groups and online, celebrating factual books. NNFN works regularly with the SLA and their Information Award, the Science Museum and other organisations.

The Jean Russell Storytelling Project: born out of the Jean Russell Gift, it not only commemorates early member Jean Russell's enthusiasm and passion but also celebrates the Federation's continuing commitment to the power of story to inspire children's imagination.

The Annual Conference: held every Spring and usually organised by a book group and the National Executive, it brings delegates together to celebrate the world of children's literature with authors, illustrators, poets, storytellers and publishers.

In recognition of the outstanding contribution that these projects and others have made to the world of children's books, individual members and the Federation itself have been presented over the years with the Eleanor Farjeon Award by the Children's Book Circle: Anne Wood in 1969, Jean Russell posthumously in 1983, Val Bierman in 1987 and the Federation of Children's Book Groups in 2011.

Foreword

Reading is solitary. Encounters between readers and books happen one at a time. When the right book reaches the right child at the right time, she or he goes into the book alone, to experience the new world or worlds it has to offer, to get the astonishing news of what this world looks like through other eyes, and when the book affects them most deeply to be changed by it, forever and ever. That's why reading is such an important act of early independence. That's why it has the deep power to persuade children that the world is wider and richer and more hopeful than it may look in the very hard places where some of them live.

But all the more reason why there should be all the support there can be to bring them to the start of this individual adventure – to provide the expertise, and the recommendations, and the physical opportunity, to begin discovering what depths there are, and what pleasures, in those quiet rectangular things made of paper. In a world where books can be outbid by louder promises, where they can seem forbidding for those who have not yet cracked the code of their power, where access to reading is too often correlated with class, the FCBG shines because it wants to help every child find the way to the doors of story. Fifty years? I hope they last another century.

Francis Spufford

Francis Spufford is the author of five highly-praised books of non-fiction, most frequently described by reviewers as either 'bizarre' or 'brilliant', and usually as both. He has been longlisted or shortlisted for prizes in science writing, historical writing, political writing, theological writing, and writing 'evoking the spirit of place'. In 2007 Francis was elected a Fellow of the Royal Society of Literature. His novel, Golden Hill, *won the Costa Book Award for a first novel in 2017, and also the Ondaatje Prize. His memoir of childhood reading,* The Child That Books Built, *is often cited in discussions about literacy strategies and cultural provision for children.*

Preface

When the National Executive first considered how to celebrate the achievements of the Federation of Children's Book Groups as it neared its 50th anniversary, the decision was taken to review the archives as a first step. It soon became clear that the charity has been a leader in the field of children's books, playing a pivotal role over its 50 years, both in the UK and internationally. With many hundreds of thousands of children benefiting from our work, it is therefore something to celebrate and to be proud of! So, a short history of the Federation was compiled, not only to highlight its influence but also to remember its many achievements from the heady days of the 1960s to the present day. Thanks to the generosity of Founder, Anne Wood, and the Ragdoll Foundation, a simple 8-page leaflet turned into a wonderfully designed book.

The Working Party learned how the Federation grew organically from *Books For Your Children* into a national charity, about the development of our national initiatives and the myriad of ways in which groups have changed the reading landscape of children's books. Federation members have brought Story Sacks to hospitals, taken books to Zambia and to Cape Town's townships, helped found Seven Stories and Book Aid International and worked with publishers, authors, illustrators, museums and festivals... there is more but you need to read the book!

We would like to thank everyone who has taken the time to talk to us, tell their stories and show their pictures, bringing the past 50 years to life. By sharing the aspirations of those who were involved in the early days, we hope we will inspire you to continue to fulfil the mission of the charity to bring children and books together and, in the process, share not only memories but also our passion and commitment to the ethos of the Federation. Maybe it will give you some new (or even old...) ideas!

History Working Party, April 2018

The Federation of Children's Book Groups

2016
The Jean Russell Storytelling Project started

2011
The Federation received The Eleanor Farjeon Award

1998
National Year of Reading Grant

1990
Story Aid Project

1980
The Children's Book Award was created

1970
First conference - Festival Hall, London

1965
Sowing the Seed: Books For Your Children

First Fifty Years

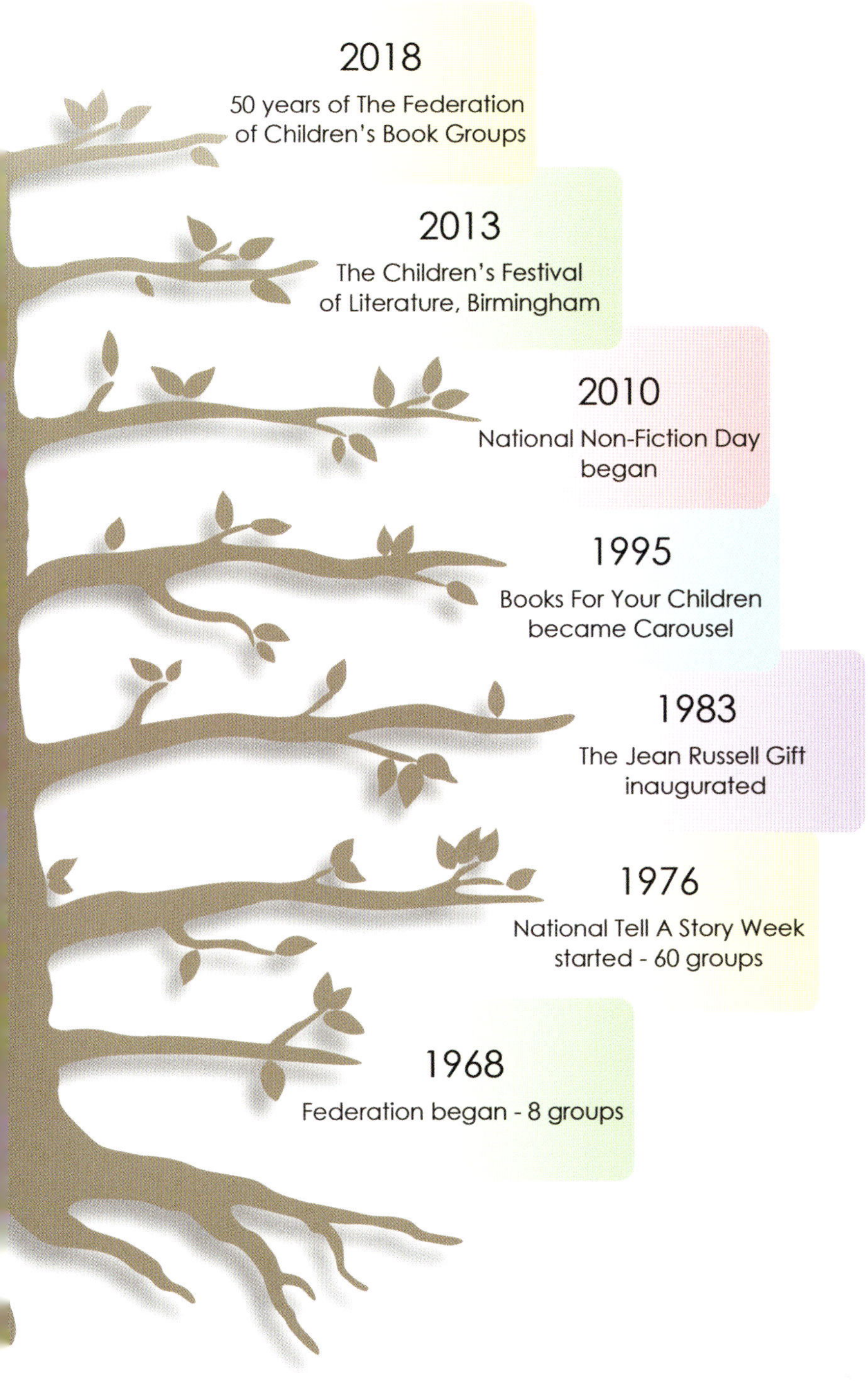

1

Preparing the Soil

Books For Your Children and the creation of the Federation.

The 1960s: Children of the Revolution The story of the Federation of Children's Book Groups (also known as the Federation or FCBG) starts in the early 1960s, a decade of upheaval and social change, a heady mix of politics, music... and a revolution in children's books. Books in general, and children's books in particular, were booming in the 1960s. Children's publishing was experiencing a golden age, as professional children's book editors started to gain influence. Chief amongst these was Kaye Webb, who joined Puffin in 1961. Her primary motivation was that children should have access to books and be entertained by them. Today this sounds self-evident, but in those days the few children's books published were in black and white and usually hardback. Books were expensive, hard to come by and precious to own. There were very few sources of information available to parents about children's books and specialist children's bookshops were rare – you could not take a small child into a bookshop! Kaye Webb, Anne Wood and the Federation changed all that.

Author and illustrator Brian Wildsmith's creativity with form and colour sparked the development of high quality, full colour picture books. He explained: "When I started there was no full colour printing, everything could only be done in three colours. This meant that I had to do a separate drawing for each colour and each drawing then had to be precisely over-printed." Times were indeed changing: in the same year that the Federation began in 1968, three seminal children's picture books were published by illustrators at the start of their brilliant careers: *Patrick* by Quentin Blake, Judith Kerr's *The Tiger Who Came to Tea* and Pat Hutchins' *Rosie's Walk*. These picture books exemplified a freedom of illustration and powerful use of colour that still resonates today.

Critically, there was not only limited access to books and to expert knowledge but also to recommendations of high quality children's books for teachers and parents. While some were fortunate to be able to visit a library, smaller towns did not have a library or, if there was one, it might not open daily or the children's section might be in a corridor or a broom cupboard. Often there was a very limited range of fiction and non-fiction. Learning to read with *Janet and John* was not inspiring and parents, teachers and librarians were united in their desire for access to more exciting material.

One source of information was Margery Fisher's magazine, *Growing Points*, first published bi-monthly in 1962. While some reviews were written by others, on the whole Margery wrote most of them herself. Aimed at parents, it gave insightful commentary on new publications across the age range. Margery's book, *Intent on Reading,* was highly influential and came to the attention of one particular individual who was also seeking to promote children reading for pleasure: Anne Wood.

Anne Wood: the Federation's driving force

Anne Wood was brought up in County Durham and qualified as a secondary school teacher at the Bingley Training College. Her first post in Spennymoor enabled her to enthuse children about reading and her school plays became a legend by involving as many of the school's pupils as possible. Once married and living in Surbiton, her second post involved children whose cultural and reading background was as impoverished as those children up north. As a result, Anne was an early pioneer of the Scholastic Children's Paperback Club and became its Editor when she left teaching after the birth of her daughter.

Books For Your Children: 'children are not ignorant' – the importance of the child's voice

In 1965, Anne Wood created the magazine *Books For Your Children,* to show parents the range of stories they could share with their own children and others, when promoting reading for pleasure and stimulating imagination. Her mission was not to endorse reading schemes or emphasise the importance of reading to enhance life chances and future success, but to share her love of stories and books for their own sake. In her own words, *Books For Your Children* will provide: "at the lowest possible cost, brief information on a wide selection of books, new developments in the children's book trade, a guide to local bookshops and forthcoming events."

The magazine gave a voice to authors and illustrators as well as concerned parents. It highlighted the beginning of the widening range of books for children, with advertisements from publishers promoting new paperbacks. Its tone was approachable and practical, enabling parents to be as selective as they wished, and its circulation grew steadily.

Anne caught the mood and concerns of parents accurately. Here is a snapshot of some of the content of *Books For Your Children* (Vol. 1 Issue 2 Jan 1966):

- a request for interested participants to join a review panel of BBC Storytime
- a listing of forthcoming radio broadcasts of children's stories
- an article by Mrs Dashwood of The Rainbow Bookshop (Walton-on-Thames) providing a list of well-tested books for reading aloud to the 4-8 age group
- Nina Bawden (author of *Carrie's War*) on the challenges of writing for children
- Experiences in one family: Mrs. Claire Clery writes of her own family experiences and stresses the importance of providing the widest possible range of books "in order to learn discernment".

BOOKS
FOR YOUR CHILDREN

A COUNTING-OUT
RHYME

Intery, mintery, cutery-corn,
Apple seed and apple thorn;
Wine, brier, limber-lock,
Five geese in a flock,
Sit and sing by a spring,
O-U-T, and in again.

Anon.

SUMMER 1968

ONE SHILLING AND SIXPENCE

Cover of Books For Your Children – Summer 1968.

Nina wrote: "no flowery or shoddy writing style, clear, unobtrusive and exact, and a tidy ending". For her, "Children differ from adults only in that they lack knowledge and experience: they are not ignorant, not intellectually simple."

Even then, the importance of the child's voice in selecting reading materials was recognised.

The first meeting

Anne Wood offered a course for parents: "*Children's books and you",* held at the Walton and Weybridge Evening Institute, which inspired a nucleus of parents, teachers and librarians to create a *Books For Your Children* group. The members found that their experiences of sharing and discussing books was of such value they should continue to meet. The Rainbow Bookshop offered a venue for this group and the first event was a talk by Kathleen Lines on *Choosing Books for Children*.

For Anne, the mission for parents was to enable their children to grow and develop by sharing stories, stimulating imagination and encouraging empathy. If the child's own critical thinking and voice is regarded as an important part of its future and character, then they need to have access to the widest range of experiences and reading materials. Anne found her views chimed with parents' worries and desires and she used this opportunity to raise the level of awareness.

Growing outwards: first groups – from Hounslow to Cheshire and beyond

Local groups started to form organically to share ideas, inspired by *Books For Your Children*. These groups were often miles from any bookshop or library, so they became licensed book agencies and sold books at author and school events. This is, of course, many years before one-click purchases online, so ease of access to book purchases was vital.

One such group was Hounslow. In the 1969-70 Yearbook, Pam Carter describes the difficulties she had in encouraging her son to read and finding the right book for him. Reading a letter from Anne Wood in the *New Scientist* magazine, deploring the lack of parental information on children's books, she was prompted to subscribe to *Books For Your Children* and she attended the first meeting at the Rainbow Bookshop. She enjoyed this so much she became a staunch supporter. Setting up a group nearer to home, she elicited help from Hounslow Children's Librarian and was offered the School Services building with a stock of 11,000 children's books as a venue.

In the same Yearbook, Jean Russell was publicising her Cheshire *Books For Your Children* group. Kaye Webb was the speaker at an event, coupled with a Puffin film on Alan Garner. The event included a 'Book Bring and Buy Sale' and copies of the latest *Books For Your Children* were available. Future events advertised included a Christmas panel event on book selection, a Christmas Book Exhibition "for parents, god-parents, grandparents to browse and *find the right book for their child"* and finally details of the next meeting of the discussion group for an evening of *chatter* about children's books (our italics).

This full programme typifies the informality and congeniality which has been the major feature of the groups from the very beginning to the present day, whilst always keeping the focus on bringing children and books together.

Anne Wood supported many of the groups by providing speakers and attending the meetings with words of encouragement and ideas.

Where did the Federation come from: the first Executive Committee
From this sharing of experience and expertise, the *Books For Your Children* groups grew from 8 groups in 1968 to 60 by 1970. While each book group remained self-determining and local in focus, in 1968 it was decided to form the first Executive Committee to manage national initiatives and create a national forum. The inaugural meeting of the Federation was held on 26th October 1968. One hundred people met in Caxton Hall in London, creating a Federation from small groups

which "can give voice to the concerns of parents and any others wishing to identify with us".

The business of creating a Federation and an Executive Committee was a morning event, while in the afternoon delegates heard from Joan Cass, a lecturer at the London Institute of Education and staunch group supporter; Charles Keeping, illustrator and Winner of the Kate Greenaway Medal 1968; Grace Hogarth, editor at Longmans Publishing; Leon Garfield, novelist and Edward Blishen, writer and educationalist, with time for questions at the end.

This combination of experts, novelists, illustrators and publishers has remained a feature of Federation Conferences, national and local, with much discussion and debate on the changing issues in children's literature.

> (The FCBG) This was very much ahead of its time.
>
> *Jonathan Stroud, Author*

'The right thing at the right time'....
The first constitution of the Federation was agreed in 1969. Three resolutions were adopted:

(1) that the Federation should become a corporate member of the National Book League (NBL) in support of the League's work
(2) that the Federation should take steps to discover the ways in which, in cooperation with the British Forces Education and Welfare authorities, they can assist in the expansion of library facilities for the children of families serving abroad and can help those families to initiate local arrangements for the purchase of children's books
(3) although no vote was taken it was decided to undertake a survey following many complaints to the Federation regarding the lack of

suitable radio programmes for children's leisure listening times, particularly the lack of storytelling and book programmes, and to consult with the NBL and other interested bodies with a view to further action.

The organisation gained charitable status in 1978.

The first National Secretary, Jennifer Robinson, said:

"Anne's enthusiasm and vision is so convincing that it seemed quite natural for group organisers from all over the country to meet in London and form the Federation of Children's Book Groups in October 1968 and the Federation Committee still looks to her for its inspiration and driving force. All this, in addition to running a home and caring for her 4-year-old daughter and a new baby, often singlehanded, since her husband's work as Secretary to the Federation of Film Societies frequently took him away from home. Talking to Anne you realise that all this activity you know about is only the tip of the iceberg: give Anne Wood carte blanche, a thousand pounds and she would do things for children's books that would make the English-speaking world sit up and take notice. The Federation is justly proud of its founder." (Newsletter no.3 November 1968)

...the passion and dedication shown by members of the Federation of Children's Book Group.

Chris Riddell, former Children's Laureate

2

Sowing the Seeds

Celebrating the strengths and diversity of our groups and members, then and now. Official recognition with the Eleanor Farjeon Award.

Anne's achievement was formally recognised when she received the Eleanor Farjeon Award in 1969.

When accepting the award, Anne said: "Books are an inevitable part of life, as inevitable for our children as teddy bears and vitamin drops. It is not so for all children. It needed the Plowden Report[1] to put into words that many children are being story starved. Schools are often hard put to equip children with basic reading skills, to see that these reading skills keep pace with children's story needs can be beyond the scope of the classroom. But it should be within the scope of every home. Here is a sphere in which parents can join with teachers and librarians without in any way conflicting with professional techniques." (1969-1970 Yearbook).

The diversity of the groups

The newly-formed Federation encouraged the book groups to share their passion for bringing children and books together, while allowing for a huge variety in location, age groups and audiences, whether in towns or villages, in schools or nurseries, hospitals or libraries.

---

1. *Plowden Report: Children and their Primary Schools, Central Advisory Council for Education (England), 1967.*

Anne Wood receives the Eleanor Farjeon Award in 1969.

The book groups reflected, and still reflect today, the interests of their own members and their geographical location, often with a specific flavour. Groups as far afield as Dundee to Pembrokeshire, Southampton to Plymouth, North Somerset to North West London, Harrogate to Lewes... all are run entirely by volunteers who share a passion for inspiring children to read and share stories.

Aldbourne Children's Book Group (CBG), formed in 1975 and based primarily around the village school, organises a float for the Carnival and children regularly share stories with older residents at the local Care Home. Volunteers make Story Sacks for the hospital in Swindon. These resources are particularly valuable in a one-to-one teaching situation, and are also often found on the ward.

Ancient Egyptian Story Sack.

Ipswich CBG, started in 1976 and Oxford CBG, started in 1993, run very successful one-day conferences, with local authors and storytellers, often around themes such as non-fiction.

In the Edinburgh newsletter January 1982, Jill McCarthy recounts a meeting of Shirley Hughes with children from Donaldson's School for the Deaf at the Mitchell Library in Glasgow and a new appreciation of the challenges facing deaf children. Although we are all aware of inclusion these days, it was innovative at that time to realise that deaf children too should be included.

Other groups are mainly community based, for example Dudley CBG, Lincs CBG and North Somerset CBG, who organise author events in schools, while South Bucks CBG and Oxted CBG are very much focused on family activities.

Aldbourne CBG mask making.

Oxford CBG National Tell-A-Story Week making musical instruments.

Rewarding and fun, then and now: from early groups to newer groups, with baseball teams, Astérix chariots, balloon races, Paddington Bear...

Pat Thomson was a founder member of the Rushden CBG in rural Northamptonshire, surrounded by what she calls "a bookless environment". She tells how the group depended on a small group of enthusiasts on the committee, yet still managed to attract crowds of 200 or more to their events.

They held two kinds of events:

- Information for parents and teachers about children's books.
- Activities for children – usually themed.

Here is a flavour of two of their most memorable activities:

- In 1976, on the theme of American Independence at the USAF base at Alconbury, officers' wives told stories of Brer Rabbit as well as sharing expertise about American children's books. The event was enhanced by the presence of the base's baseball team!

- On a transport theme the group had a brainwave: why not ask Macmillan for their Astérix chariot? Brought up by a willing husband from London, the event was boosted by tug-of-war teams who wore horned helmets and blonde plaits.

The group also set up a book agency, as did many of the early groups located in areas with no bookshops. The nearest bookshop, based in Northampton, used to provide them with books on a Sale or Return basis and then used the children's views to build their own lists!

The Edinburgh CBG newsletter of March 1984 explains at length how to set up a book agency. Their activities fall into 4 categories; talks to adults about children's books with a selection of titles on sale; author

An early book group committee meeting at Rushden.

events in schools; providing a book stall at members' meetings and supplying book boxes for schools and nursery groups for mothers and teachers to browse and buy.

Another early group was based in Formby, Merseyside, run by Liz Youngs.

Formby CBG flourished from 1980 to 1993. Members were mainly families with young children and teachers who organised lots of activities for local children: regular story times at the local library, book fairs, competitions, parties and a Story Tent at the annual summer Formby Show. There were visits from Spot the Dog, Peter Rabbit and Paddington Bear, and young booklovers were able to meet favourite authors. During Children's Book Week in 1988 a balloon race took place – with book token prizes – and the group joined with Cheshire CBG in 1990 to organise the Annual Federation Conference at Chester College with the theme 'Yesterday, Today, Forever'. Liz says: "It was a very rewarding activity for me and a way to become part of the local community."

To be at a gathering of members of the FCGB is to instantly be among friends. The love members have for children's books is infectious – and their wide knowledge of their subject is a great resource.

Nick Butterworth, Author and Illustrator

Today it is still highly rewarding for adults and children to be part of a children's book group. Kate West, member of Reading CBG, says:

"I first joined the FCBG with my young daughters as a way to bring more books into the house and discover new authors. We then realised how much fun it was to vote for the books in the Children's Book Award and my girls loved the knowledge that their opinions counted. Encouraging our school to become involved, I have seen the enjoyment it has brought children who don't have a wide range of books at home. What a brilliant way not only to bring children and books together, but also to create and develop a passion for reading and literacy in a generation bombarded with technology."

Spotlight on some of the long-standing groups

Ipswich CBG

Ipswich CBG has been bringing children and books together for over 40 years. All their members have done whatever it takes to inspire a love of reading in children, from hosting book parties, to standing in rain-swept fields, to donning character costumes on very hot days. Ipswich also supports local charities and other organisations, such as the education room at Ipswich Hospital, with gifts of books. Events have

Ipswich CBG celebrating National Tell-A-Story Week.

included story times, book fairs, quizzes, competitions, book launches and talks from leading authors and illustrators. Ipswich is proud to have hosted two successful national conferences, in 2003 at Southwold and 2013 at Culford School, as well as two one-day conferences: 'Picturing the Past', about historical fiction for children, and 'Adventures in the Real World', exploring information books. Membership includes schools, libraries, booksellers, local authors and illustrators as well as families.

> The Federation of Children's Book Groups... in their own quiet and single-minded way, they've done more for literacy, for literature and for reading than almost anyone.
>
> *Anthony Horowitz, Author and Screenwriter*

Birmingham CBG

David Blanch became aware of children's book groups when he started teaching in Norfolk and was given a copy of *Books For Your Children*. On moving to Birmingham in 1969, he started a group and was subsequently invited onto the National Executive as Membership Officer "as the only man!"

In 1993 North and South Birmingham CBG organised the Federation's Silver Jubilee Conference and it was for this celebration that the Federation commissioned Mick Inkpen to design a new logo (FED TED), which is still in use today.

The FCBG logo.

Over the years Birmingham has continued to organise school book fairs, book swaps, author visits and a

Knockout Quiz for primary school children, that tested their knowledge of books. The group also supports local community events: Summer fairs, festivals, even entering a dragon in a local scarecrow event based on children's book characters.

Our individual and professional members

As well as book groups springing up around the country, individual and professional members have also brought their own expertise and enthusiasm to the Federation. Many authors, illustrators, librarians, bookshops and schools have supported the Federation over the last 50 years. They have been particularly influential in bringing children and books together through author events and signings, supporting many national initiatives and bringing the ethos of the Federation into their working practices.

Individual members are usually people who do not live near a local group.

Individual member, Clare Zinkin, had her first contact with the Federation through the website. She says: "I have worked in children's publishing as an editor for years, but in 2014 was branching out into working with schools and parents to make sure children had access to books, and could find a way to love reading. The FCBG fitted perfectly with these aims. I joined one of their local book groups for a time, then attended the Children's Book Award Ceremony and the Annual Conference, and before long was fully ensconced in the charity.

For me, the FCBG ticks the boxes. I was after a group that focused on encouraging children to read for pleasure: to bring children and books together in a fun way. It's also completely open to all, there is no exclusivity to the FCBG, you just need to love books."

Professional members include authors, booksellers, illustrators, poets, publishers, schools and storytellers.

Retired children's bookseller, Karen Hellewell, found that becoming a member of the Federation gives any bookseller greater insight into the choices made by the children. Karen says: "You can focus on the up-and-coming talent as well as on the children's classics. As the owner of The Well Wisher specialist children's bookshop in Devizes, I worked closely with the Federation for many years. I attended my first conference at Marlborough where I met the incomparable Shirley Hughes and I have been a staunch supporter from then on. I know that there is the right book for every child; you just have to find it and the work that the Federation does is pivotal in this."

Jonathan Stroud, children's author and son of St Albans CBG member, remembers the Federation clearly: "My debt goes right back into the murky past, to my childhood in the late 1970s. Membership of the FCBG creates opportunities for the child to enjoy the space and setting to come face to face with magic."

3

Seedlings Growing

The start of National Tell-A-Story Week, the Federation's involvement in Butlin's Venture Weeks, lobbying the BBC, Conferences UK-wide, the first anthology.

During the first decade of the Federation many national initiatives sprang up, often around the theme of sharing stories, as the Federation found its national voice.

National Tell-A-Story Week was created in 1976. Usually held during a specific week in May, each book group celebrated story in their own way with national competitions and special events involving many well-known names.

In those early days the Federation didn't lack ambition! NTASW was celebrated on BBC Nationwide and in 1977 four children's book groups from the Midlands hired a train to take 500 adults and children, authors and illustrators to Paddington, followed by coaches to take them to the Embankment. After a picnic lunch, the children were led in procession across Westminster Bridge by a Pearly King and Queen with Gyles Brandreth, dressed as a jester, doing cartwheels, to the National Theatre. The rest of the day was spent listening to the many authors and illustrators who had come to entertain the children.

Stop Off For A Story with Gyles Brandreth as the court jester in 1977.

Now National Share-A-Story Month (NSSM) covers the whole of May and the website contains useful downloadable packs of resources.

Lobbying the BBC. The first national initiative was the mobilisation of the rapidly growing number of book groups to encourage the BBC to reconsider their cut backs on children's radio in 1969, with members writing to the BBC Controller. Their voice was heard, with a response being received from the then Controller of Radio 4.

The National Conferences gave book groups the opportunity to meet each other and share ideas for children's activities. Held annually, the conference changed location throughout the UK, with the 10th Birthday held in Edinburgh and quickly became a popular and well-respected annual event.

Butlin's Venture Weeks for school children was initiated in 1972 by Paul Winterforde-Young, a senior executive at Butlin's, working with

David Blanch. Federation book group volunteers manned and ran a 'Story Room', a quiet refuge during the day for children to enjoy reading, share stories and talk about the books they liked, with evening storytelling sessions. Volunteers worked in Minehead, Bognor and Barry Island for many years and Butlin's were pleased to use it as training for their Redcoats.

Butlin's Story Room.

The FCBG is an excellent, energetic and enthusiastic organisation, determined to encourage children to delight in the joys of reading.

Jacqueline Wilson, Dame and former Children's Laureate

The First Anthology: *Stories for Children* 1976

The Federation's first anthology was compiled by Anne Wood, containing stories selected by families for reading aloud. This revolutionary approach was to test each story with children through the book groups, therefore giving children a part to play and their own voice in the compilation. A range of anthologies have been created since, all based on the same key principle. Each story was timed and the selection ranged from classics such as *Pippi Longstocking*, chosen by Minehead CBG and the Pecorelli family, and *The Iron Man,* selected by Sheffield CBG and the Short family, to new material such as *Little Polly Riding Hood* chosen by the Wolsingham CBG, the Turner family and Pat Triggs.

Appendix A gives a list of all the published anthologies.

Throughout this decade, book groups flourished amidst a wide range of activities: puppet workshops, weekend conferences, storytelling in hospitals, book selling, Scandinavian evenings, teddy bear picnics, local carnivals and even a Great Womble Hunt.

Right: Stories for Children cover, 1976.

4

Sturdy Shoots

The creation of the Children's Book Award, the Jean Russell Gift and the regular publication of anthologies, newsletter and booklists. The Federation also developed many links at home and abroad.

Despite the crash of the early 1980s, which led to big changes in publishing as the early professional children's editors moved on (Kaye Webb left the Puffin Club in 1981), there was an increased focus on the bottom line and a reduced stock holding at publishers, the Federation continued to flourish and developed more national initiatives and publications, all of which have stood the test of time.

The Children's Book Award: involving the children throughout

In 1980 Pat Thomson conceived the idea of creating an entirely new book award that actually involved children throughout the process. Similar awards were given on behalf of librarians or publishers, but no other major children's award involved solely children as judges. Publishers donated books to ten of the Federation's book groups, covering the whole of the UK. These 'Testing Groups' developed a network of schools and families who read the books then completed a simple review form. The results were tabulated centrally and a winner emerged. From these results, the Federation published a *Pick of the Year* booklist, an annotated list of the top 50 titles. The Award Ceremony was celebrated with a lunch to which shortlisted authors and illustrators, their publishers and most importantly, children from the

Testing Groups were invited. Each of the shortlisted authors received a portfolio of letters and pictures from the children. The Award later obtained sponsorship from the Save and Prosper Educational Trust, negotiated by Jenny Blanch. At this stage the prize varied each year. In 1987 Allan and Janet Ahlberg were presented with a post-box, for *The Jolly Postman.* From 1989 onwards, the Overall Winner has received a wonderful silver 'oak tree' trophy created by royal silversmith, Graham Stewart. The Category Winners' prizes and the Older Readers Category were introduced in 1990. The award was subsequently supported by the Paul Hamlyn Foundation.

Children's Book Award silver trophy, created by Graham Stewart.

Bob Swindells remembers:
"Winning the Children's Book Award in 1985 felt terrific. The ceremony itself in those early, unsponsored days was conducted in a tent, in a park in Nottingham. It was raining but I couldn't have felt more euphoric if we had been doing it in the Royal Albert Hall. Brenda and I sang a peace song called *Let It Begin With Me* which I accompanied with simple guitar chords, as we did back then. That gorgeous oak and silver trophy was still in the future, but the folio of children's letters that marked my win was as precious to me as any trophy. It still is.

I won again in 1990 and this time there was a swanky venue and the trophy but all of that couldn't equal the joy I felt in that damp little tent in Nottingham. Nothing ever will."

...the huge contribution the organisation has made to the vital work of bringing children and books together.

Robert Swindells, Author and Children's Book Award Winner

Jean Russell and the Jean Russell Gift: Anyone for the biggest jelly party in the world?
Jean was the Co-Editor of *Books For Your Children* from 1977 until 1983 and the first Editor of the Federation newsletter. Her ambition was to hold the biggest jelly party in the world in the Royal Albert Hall, sadly not fulfilled since she suffered from asthma all her life and died very suddenly in 1983. Anne Wood describes her thus,

"Despite, or perhaps because of, her disability, Jean gave unstintingly of her love and time in bringing children and good books together. She knew how much stories could mean to children in moments of pain and stress as well as in shared moments within a loving family situation."
(Books For Your Children, Spring 1983)

"Invariably warm and wonderfully encouraging, with Jean, people always came away with the feeling that devoting so much time to children's books had been exactly the right decision," Pat Thomson.

Passionate about stories and books, Jean was a feisty woman with energy and dynamism.

Brenda Swindells said, "There was Jean Russell, a tiny person whose lifelong affliction was totally eclipsed by her enthusiasm and vivacity."

She received the Eleanor Farjeon Award posthumously for her energy and enthusiasm for bringing stories to all children. Anne Wood set up the Jean Russell Gift in memory of her friend, which, at the time, comprised a donation of books to a handicapped child nominated by a group member. It has since evolved into the Jean Russell Storytelling Project.

Jean Russell.

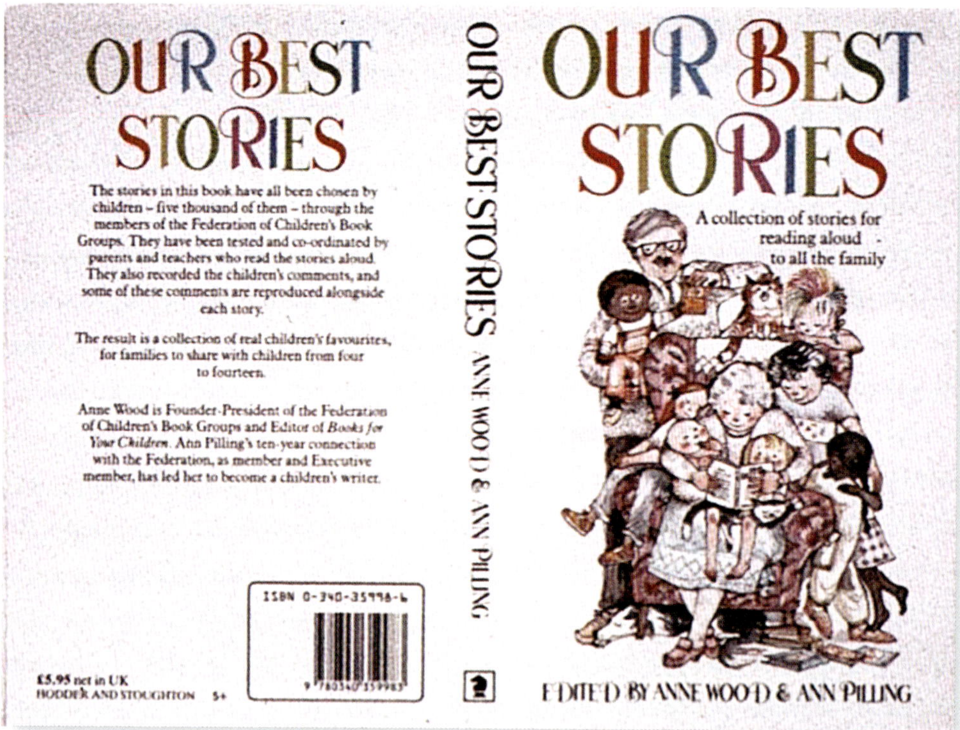

Our Best Stories anthology, 1986.

New publications

1986 saw the publication of the second anthology, *Our Best Stories,* edited by Anne Wood and Ann Pilling, in which all the stories were rigorously tested (as before) by children from 45 children's book groups around the UK. The stories were divided into age ranges and an appendix indicated other books by the chosen authors. The anthology combined well known British authors such as Ted Hughes and Philippa Pearce with others from overseas such as R.N. Munsch, Margaret Mahy and Leila Berg.

Booklists

The Federation has been producing booklists for many years. They have always been distributed free of charge. Compiled by members and tested by children they have traditionally been show-cased at the

Annual Conference. Now available to download from the website, they cover a wide age-range, from 0-21 (or older!), and include non-fiction, poetry, genre and graphic novels. The booklists support and extend resources available to parents and carers who are looking for alternate ways to encourage and inspire their children with reading. Visit Appendix B to see a list of Booklists.

...an idea of brilliant simplicity – bringing children to good books and good books to children in the most imaginative ways.

Elizabeth Laird, Author and Children's Book Award Winner

Newsletter

The Federation newsletter started in the early 1970s. From its beginning as a typed, stencilled and stapled page of news to the current 8 page full colour, printed magazine, it has adapted and changed as technology has improved and its audiences and contributors have become more diverse. However, it still retains the distinctive voice of the Federation, giving groups an opportunity to celebrate their events, along with our national initiatives and projects.

Development of International Links

1979 was the International Year of the Child and Val Bierman, founder member of the Edinburgh CBG, established a link with Choma Library in Zambia, organising the collection and donation of books through book groups. She developed the children's section of the Edinburgh Festival – when there were no children's events nor even much of a focus on books. Now we take for granted that children's events are integral to most festivals, but then it was very new, and she was interviewed by student Ian Rankin for an article in the *Festival Times*. Val Bierman also set up the Kathleen Fidler Award for promising young Scottish writers.

She received the Eleanor Farjeon Award for her work in 1987. For Val, as for many others then and now, the Federation meant pleasure and friendship, sharing a passion for children's books and for bringing children and books together.

The Edinburgh group also created a travelling exhibition of books on diversity, covering a wide range of ages and ethnicities which were loaned to schools that needed them. This demonstrates the forward thinking of the Federation members who realised the importance of raising awareness with parents, teachers and librarians. Pat Thomson commented on the current concern with the lack of diversity in publishing and children's books today, “Here we are re-inventing the wheel again. The Federation was already there.”

And throughout this period the number of book groups continued to expand with new groups in the UK as well as in Christchurch (NZ), who twinned with Lewes in 1980. Groups in Gibraltar, Guernsey, France and New York joined the Federation in 1981.

5

First Buds Flowering: Children's Book Award Winners 1981-2017

"Special beyond words": A celebration of the only national award voted for entirely by the children.

Pat Thomson, who created the Children's Book Award in 1980, said: "We only exist to bring children and books together so any Award would need to involve them. Not just involve them, in fact. Anyone can run a few of the books past the kids. They would have to be at the heart of it... Everywhere we heard of cuts in spending on books in libraries and schools and rumours of crises... It seemed that children's fiction was an easy target. It was an act of faith, an act of solidarity with all the authors, illustrators and children's publishers."

This 'act of faith' has continued and grown, still generously supported by the publishers and still valued by the Winners. Over nearly 40 years, the Winners have reflected the wisdom and discernment of the children: authors whose books have often become classics: Roald Dahl, Jacqueline Wilson, Michael Morpurgo, J.K. Rowling...

In this chapter we celebrate all the Winners. How many have you read?

1981 ***Mr. Magnolia*** Written and illustrated by Quentin Blake (pub Red Fox)

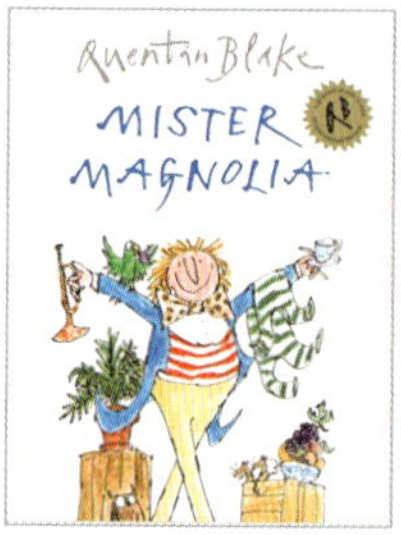

Quentin Blake's wonderfully zany and colourful illustrations and rhyming text describe the adventures of Mr Magnolia who sadly only has one boot. Frogs and newts, parakeets and owls and even a dinosaur join him in the hunt. A rollicking family favourite.

1982 ***Fair's Fair*** Written by Leon Garfield (pub Wayland, Hachette)

Jackson is cold and starving in the dreadful winter weather. He's looking forward to the steaming pie that is payment for a long night's work. When the huge black dog comes – growling and glaring – Jackson gives it half his meal. One bargain soon leads to another – and to some unexpected rewards. With an engaging (and very creepy) story, illustrated in colour and black and white on every double page spread, this story is ideal for newly confident readers.

1983 ***The BFG*** Written by Roald Dahl, illustrated by Quentin Blake (pub Puffin)

A little girl called Sophie is lying in bed in an orphanage unable to sleep when she sees a strange giant with a bag... so starts one of Roald Dahl's most well-loved adventures. We follow Sophie and the Big Friendly Giant as they catch dreams to pass on to good children and destroy nightmares. But it all goes wrong when they tangle with Fleshlumpeater, requiring a night-time visit to the Queen of England and the involvement of helicopters before the BFG and Sophie can settle in their small cottage to live happily ever after. Beautifully illustrated, this book is a children's classic.

1984 *Erik the Viking* Written by Terry Jones and illustrated by Michael Foreman (pub Puffin)

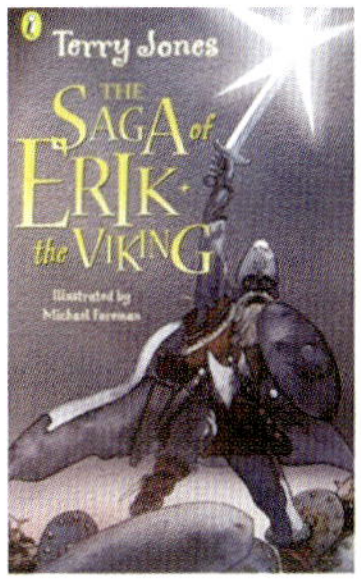

Erik and his crew from the Golden Dragon are searching for adventure in the land where the sun goes down at night. But they find more than they bargained for and their courage and skill are tested to the extremes. Will Erik win through storms, giants, enchantments and trolls to find what he seeks? Michael Foreman's wonderful illustrations add splendour to this mythical tale.

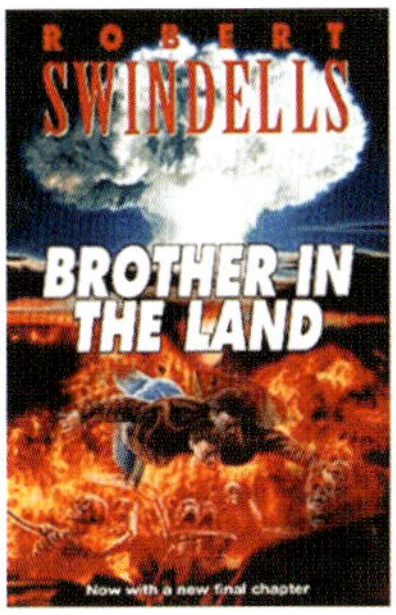

1985 *Brother in the Land* Written by Robert Swindells (pub Puffin)

A deeply moving tale of life after a nuclear bomb falls on England, the story follows teenage Danny, his younger brother Ben and a girl called Kim, who have to fight for survival in a world that has been destroyed. Robert Swindells does not flinch from describing an environment where human nature is laid bare and authority has disappeared in a land of lawlessness and gang warfare. Will they all survive? This is a powerful novel set in the ordinary town of Shipley in the north of England.

1986 *Who Wants Arthur?* Written by Amanda Graham and illustrated by Donna Erynell (pub Gareth Stevens)

Arthur is an ordinary brown dog who lives in Mrs. Humbert's Pet Shop. All he wants is to have a home. So he tries everything he can to persuade someone to take him on. He becomes a rabbit, a snake, even a fish, before he realises that he can be a success just as himself. This appeals to all children who understand what it means to want to be popular and the need to be chosen. The comedy is slapstick and the theme simple but there is a deeper content here that children respond to.

1987 ***The Jolly Postman*** Written and illustrated by Allan and Janet Ahlberg (pub Puffin)

This wonderfully witty, interactive picture book is told in jaunty rhyme. Accompanied by exquisite water-colour illustrations, the book contains a collection of letters, leaflets and cards from a variety of fairy-tale characters, which can all be taken out of the integral envelopes to read. A veritable masterpiece of storytelling!

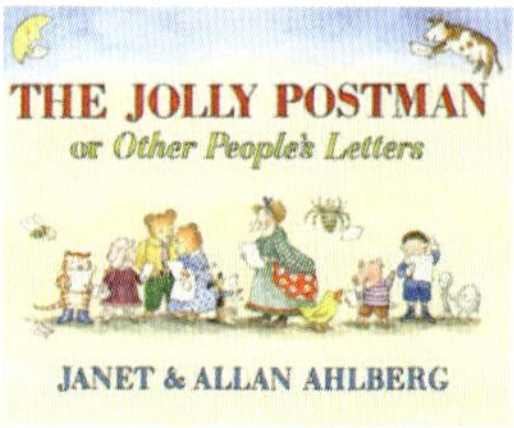

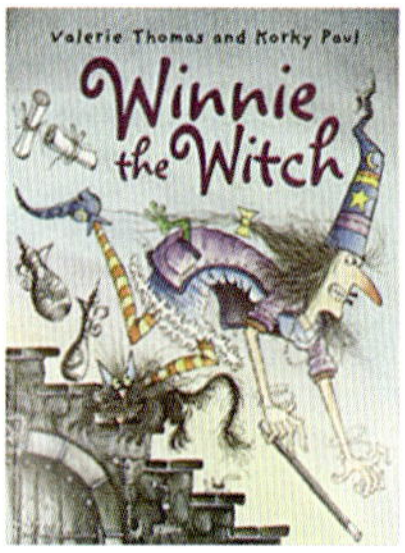

1988 ***Winnie the Witch*** Written by Valerie Thomas and illustrated by Korky Paul (pub OUP)

Winnie the Witch lives in a black house with black furnishings and Wilbur, her black cat, which can cause problems. Her attempts to solve the difficulty by casting spells on Wilbur are not terribly successful until she comes up with the perfect solution. The first in a much-loved series.

1989 ***Matilda*** Written by Roald Dahl and illustrated by Quentin Blake (pub Puffin)

This well-loved tale of a precocious child, who bests the bullying Head Miss Trunchbull and ends up happy ever after living with her favourite teacher Miss Honey, appeals to children (and adults) of all ages. Roald Dahl is a master storyteller, who understands the world of a child with all its strange, chaotic, incomprehensible and splendid possibilities and *Matilda* remains an all-time favourite.

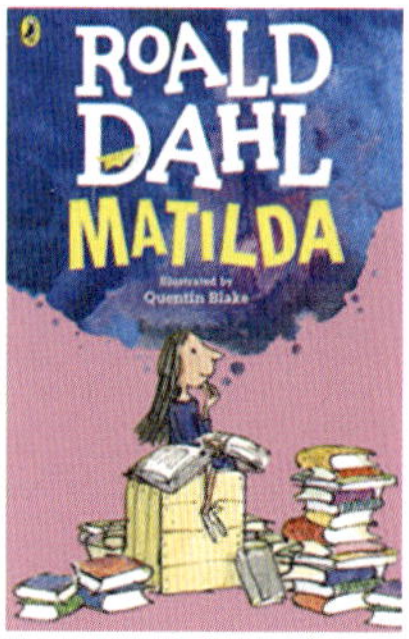

1990 ***Room 13*** Written by Robert Swindells (pub Puffin)

Fliss Morgan and her friends are on a school trip with a difference when they stay in a creepy guest house in Whitby. Every night Ellie-May Sutherland is drawn to the landing outside the mysterious Room 13. Who is staying there? Fliss and her friends attempt to unravel the identity of the room's sinister inhabitant in a story that is satisfyingly full of suspense, thrills and horror.

1991 ***Threadbear*** Written and illustrated by Mick Inkpen (pub Hodder)

There is one thing that has always been wrong with Threadbear. In his tummy is a squeaker that has never squeaked... Can Father Christmas make his wish come true and give him a squeaky tummy or will it be something much more simple that grants him his wish? With fantastic fold-out pages this picture book is a well-loved classic.

1992 ***Kiss the Dust*** Written by Elizabeth Laird (pub Macmillan)

Kiss the Dust is a compulsively readable, utterly gripping and harrowing story about the devastating effects of Saddam Hussein's genocide of the Kurds in Iraq. Tara is an ordinary teenager in Kurdistan, whose life is turned upside down when the war reaches her home. Fleeing into the mountains with only the items they can carry, Tara's family is torn apart as they struggle on a long journey to find somewhere they can call home again. This book remains in the mind of the reader long after the last page has been read.

1993 *The Suitcase Kid* Written by Jacqueline Wilson and illustrated by Nick Sharratt (pub Doubleday)

Andy had always lived in Mulberry Cottage with Mum, Dad and Radish her rabbit. But now Mum has a new home with Bill the Baboon and his three children and Dad lives with Carrie and the twins. Andy lives out of a suitcase, shuttling between the two, when all she wants to do is go back to Mulberry Cottage. There is no easy resolution to an all-too-familiar family tale, but when Andy finally realises that she is still loved and even liked – and that she likes her new families too – she learns to accept and adapt to her new life.

1994 *The Boy in the Bubble* Written by Ian Strachan (pub Mammoth)

Adam has an immune deficiency which forces him to live his life in an oxygen tent – the 'bubble' of the title. As part of a school project, Anne is forced to visit him, leading her to choose him as a 'project'. From these unlikely beginnings a tender love story develops, even though the two can't touch. When Adam is offered a bone marrow transplant to allow his immune deficiency to be corrected, the reader is taken on a roller coaster ride of emotion.

1995 *Harriet's Hare* Written and illustrated by Dick King-Smith (pub Yearling, now Penguin Random House)

Hares don't talk. Everyone knows that. But the hare Harriet meets one morning in a corn circle in her father's wheat field is a very unusual hare: a visitor from the far-off planet Pars, come to spend his holidays on Earth in the form of a talking hare. Wiz, as Harriet names her magical new friend, can speak any language, transform himself into any shape and, as the summer draws to its close, he has one last, lovely surprise in store for Harriet...

1996 ***Double Act*** Written by Jacqueline Wilson and illustrated by Nick Sharratt (pub Doubleday)

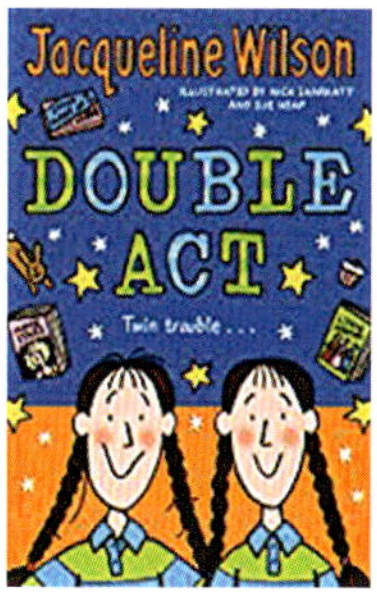

Jacqueline Wilson's second winner is written in the style of a diary, featuring identical twins Ruby and Garnet. Ruby and Garnet love each other dearly but they are completely different. Ruby is loud, outgoing and wild and Garnet is shy, quiet and kind. Ruby wants to audition to be on television, whereas Garnet wants to go to school and have a quiet life. After many arguments and fights, Ruby realises that she and Garnet do not need to be the same, and do not have to do the same things, to be happy. And they both realise that they can still be together, while apart, as long as they remember each other.

1997 ***The Hundred-Mile-an-Hour Dog*** Written by Jeremy Strong (pub Puffin)

Trevor's mum has offered him £30 to walk the dog every day of the holidays. But Streaker is no ordinary dog, she's a rocket on four legs with a woof attached! Trevor enlists the help of best friend Tina to keep Streaker under control and to train her by the end of the summer. If he fails he will lose his bet with horrible Charlie Smugg, and something very, very yucky involving frogspawn will happen. This fast-paced, laugh-out-loud book has become a classic for confident early readers.

1998 ***Harry Potter and the Philosopher's Stone*** Written by J.K. Rowling (pub Bloomsbury)

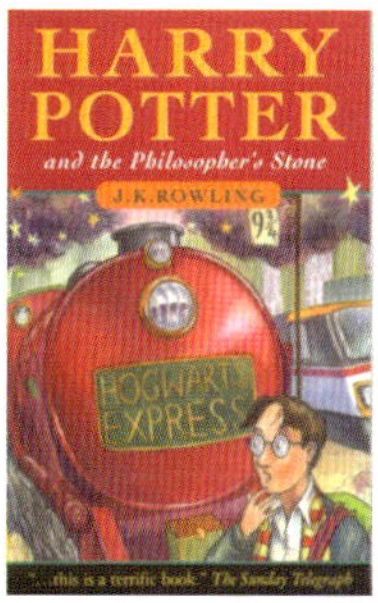

Discovering that he is a wizard is just the beginning for Harry Potter. Learning his craft and finding true friends at Hogwarts School, he must also battle against Voldemort to save everything he holds dear. Fantasy, magic and adventure combine in a series which has entranced the world. The first of the series, this book introduces the reader to the magical world of Harry, Ron and Hermione.

1999 ***Harry Potter and the Chamber of Secrets*** Written by J.K. Rowling (pub Bloomsbury)

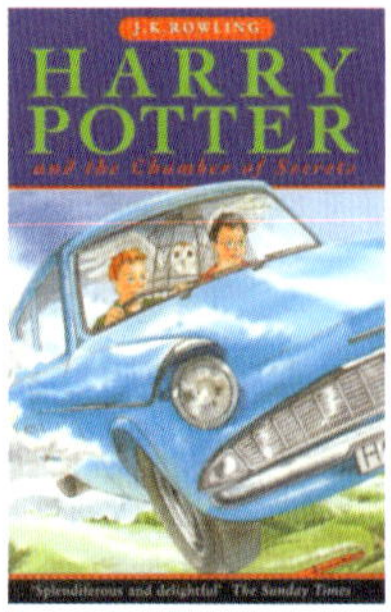

Full of magic, humour and evil, in the form of the Basilisk, the second book in the series was another worthy winner, as J.K. Rowling brought in new characters and deepened the reader's knowledge of Harry's world, scattering clues that are critical to the development of the series and its culmination with *Harry Potter and the Deathly Hallows*.

2000 ***Kensuke's Kingdom*** Written by Michael Morpurgo and illustrated by Michael Foreman (pub Egmont)

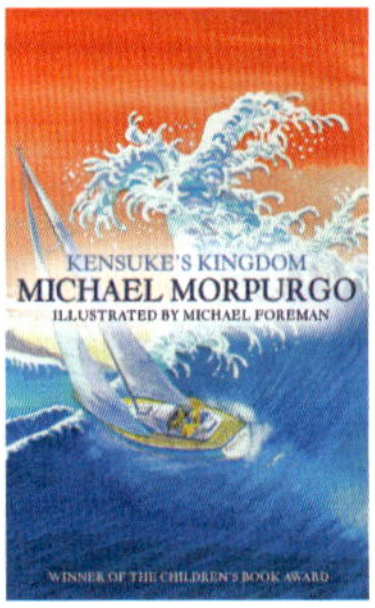

When Michael is shipwrecked alone on a Pacific island he struggles to survive until he realises that someone is watching after him. After a close call with a poisonous jelly fish, the mysterious Kensuke lets Michael into his life until Michael can return home. A poignant desert island story about loyalty and friendship.

2001 ***Eat Your Peas*** Written by Kes Gray and illustrated by Nick Sharratt (pub Red Fox)

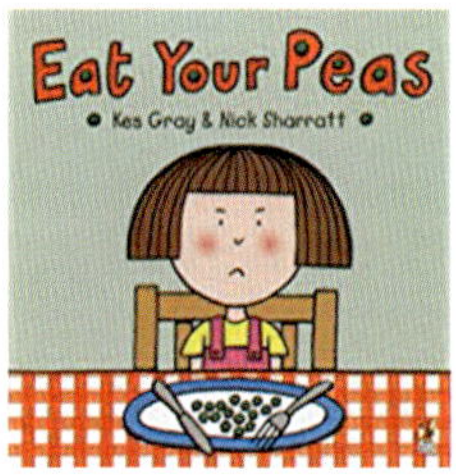

It was dinner time again and Daisy just knew what her mum was going to say, even before she said it. "Eat your peas," said Mum. "I don't like peas." said Daisy. And so the battle of wills begins. What does Mum have to promise to get Daisy to eat her peas? An extra pudding, a chocolate factory or a space rocket with double retro laser blammers? "I'll eat my peas if you eat Brussel sprouts" says Daisy. Who will win? A book everyone can appreciate, enlivened by Nick Sharratt's matchless illustrations.

2002 ***Noughts and Crosses*** Written by Malorie Blackman (pub Random House)

Set in a dystopian fictional world, where Crosses (black people like Sephy) enjoy the wealth and power in society and Noughts (white people like Callum) are second class citizens, this series for young adults is both a love story and an exploration of our role in the fight for justice in an unfair world.

2003 ***Skeleton Key*** Written by Anthony Horowitz (pub Walker)

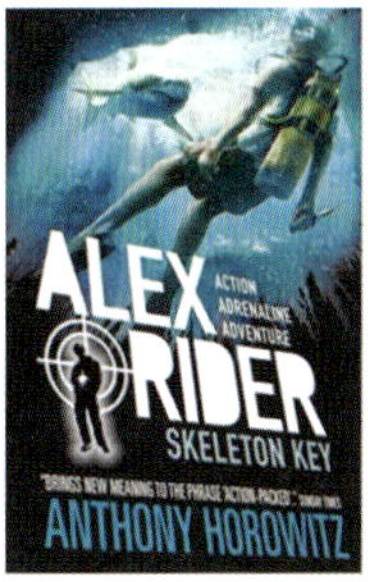

The third novel in Anthony Horowitz's fast-paced Alex Rider adventure series, sees superspy Alex battling to save the world once more, in a terrifying chain of events involving Chinese Triad gangs in London and undercover agents in Cuba. As Alex begins to make connections between an illegal nuclear weapons deal and his host, Russian General Sarov, the future of the world is at stake. As always, with Anthony Horowitz, the book proves impossible to put down.

2004 ***Private Peaceful*** Written by Michael Morpurgo (pub HarperCollins)

This deeply moving account of the horrors of the First World War is a book for all ages; for adults as well as for children. The story follows twenty-four hours at the front with Private Tommo Peaceful, whilst exploring memories of his family and life in his village back home. A compelling evocation of a traumatic time, it succeeds both as a love story and as a homage to all the young teenagers who left home to go to the trenches in World War One.

2005 ***Baby Brains*** Written and illustrated by Simon James (pub Walker)

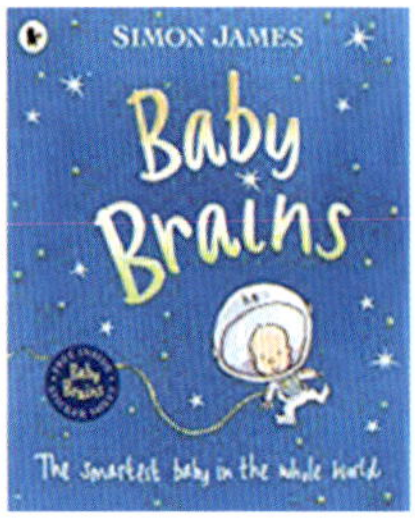

Baby Brains is an extraordinary baby who, at the age of only two weeks, mends the car, reads the paper and works as a doctor at the local hospital. But when some scientists ask him to go on the next space mission he shows that in one way at least he is just like any other baby: he wants his mummy! The perfect antidote for parents who feel pressurised to keep up with other parents, Simon James' joyous illustrations set off the witty, gentle story to perfection.

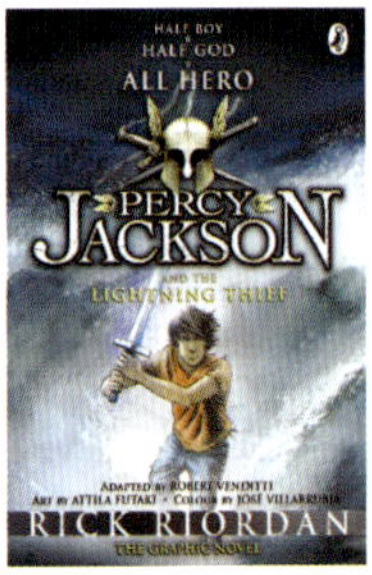

2006 ***Percy Jackson and the Lightning Thief*** Written by Rick Riordan (pub Puffin)

A series popular with young teens, in which the eponymous hero triumphs as the demigod son of Poseidon in Riordan's invented Greek mythological battles. Camp Half-Blood is a magical blend of school and demigod training camp where Percy grows into his hero role alongside an imaginative range of peers, including a satyr and a daughter of Athena. This is the first book in a thrilling series, where the story moves at a compelling pace from 21st century school outings to the gates of the Underworld itself.

2007 ***You're a Bad Man, Mr. Gum!*** Written by Andy Stanton (pub Egmont)

There is more than a nod to Past Winner, Roald Dahl, in this darkly humorous story about a man who hates children and fun and... corn on the cob. Younger Readers love this tale that also features a horrible butcher and a dastardly plot to do away with the village dog, Jake, who ruins Mr. Gum's beautiful tidy flowery garden. Can the lovely Polly, with hair like cat's daydream and who is good and true, foil Mr. Gum, save Jake and prove why truth is... a lemon meringue? Children and their parents adore the silliness and quirkiness of the first in the Mr. Gum series.

2008 ***Skulduggery Pleasant*** Written by Derek Landy (pub HarperCollins)

Stephanie's uncle Gordon is a writer of horror fiction, but when he dies and leaves her his estate, Stephanie is pursued by evil forces intent on recovering a mysterious key. She finds help from an unusual source – the wisecracking skeleton of a dead wizard. Will evil win the day? Will Stephanie and Skulduggery stop bickering long enough to stop it? This witty and dry-humoured novel is also tense and thrilling – a winning combination for older readers.

2009 ***Blood Ties*** Written by Sophie McKenzie (pub Simon and Schuster)

A gripping thriller, this novel explores the issues of genetic engineering and personal identity. Tightly plotted from the start, the main characters, Rachel and Theo, who both struggle with their sense of identity, are highly appealing to the older reader age group. The novel is fast-paced, keeping readers on the edge of their seats as the protagonists race to survive against the odds.

2010 ***The Hunger Games*** Written by Suzanne Collins (pub Scholastic)

It's the near future and a terrifying reality television show is taking place. Twelve boys and twelve girls are forced to take part in a live event called the Hunger Games. There is only one rule: kill or be killed. Sixteen-year-old Katniss has promised to take her sister's place but sees it as a death sentence. Will she manage to stay alive? Unsettling and totally gripping, this novel is the first in a globally successful trilogy.

2011 ***Shadow*** Written by Michael Morpurgo and illustrated by Christian Birmingham (pub HarperCollins)

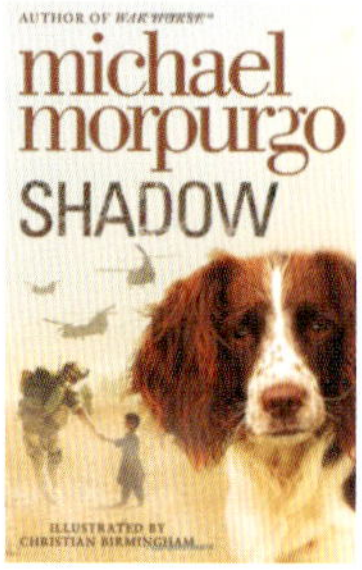

This is the story of Aman, a boy from Afghanistan who is befriended by a dog when he is fleeing the horror of war. The dog, Shadow, never leaves his side and it soon becomes clear that the destinies of Aman and Shadow are linked and always will be. Michael Morpurgo wrote this as a result of his passion for the subject: the detention centres and suffering of war, and the children appreciating the harrowing truths as revealed in this beautifully written and illustrated story.

2012 ***A Monster Calls*** Written by Patrick Ness from an idea by Siobhan Dowd and illustrated by Jim Kay (pub Walker)

The monster showed up at midnight. In this haunting and compelling story a boy tries to come to terms with his mum's illness, symbolised by the monster rising from the earth to bring the scariness of his situation right into Conor's home. But what does the monster want from Conor? The answer is: the most dangerous thing of all – the truth. Beautifully written, with outstanding illustrations, this unforgettable novel lingers in the mind.

2013 ***The Spooky Spooky House*** Written by Andrew Weale and illustrated by Lee Wildish (pub Corgi)

With a tantalising storyline, that dares the reader to explore a monstrous mansion, this spooky new take on the classic Haunted House concept is completely engrossing. It is jam-packed with lots of petrifying pop-ups and fantastic flaps to lift and on the final page there is a terrific twist. A great book for younger children to enjoy.

2014 ***The Fifth Wave*** Written by Rick Yancey (pub Penguin)

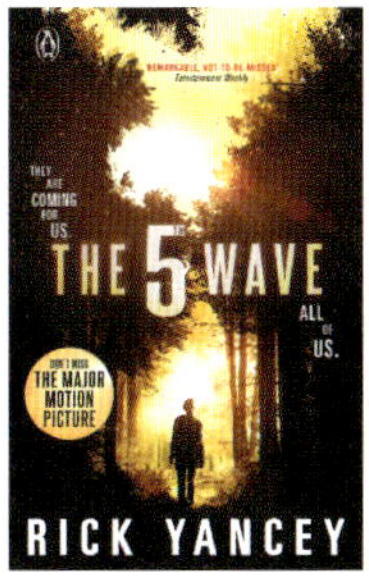

Partly inspired by leading physicist Stephen Hawking, the arrival of a massive alien spaceship is followed by waves of destruction: an electromagnetic pulse, a global tsunami, a deadly virus and then body-snatched humans. The ominous fifth wave of the title is revealed later in the book. This thrilling science fiction novel follows 16 year-old Cassie Sullivan's struggle to survive against the odds. A hugely popular choice among older voters, the book has earned Rick Yancey widespread critical acclaim.

2015 ***The Day the Crayons Quit*** Written by Drew Daywalt and illustrated by Oliver Jeffers (pub HarperCollins)

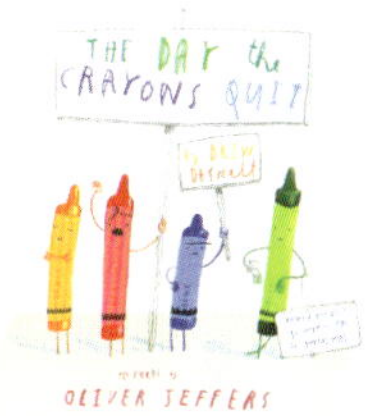

Duncan just wants to do some colouring, but when he opens his box of crayons, he has a surprise. They have all quit! In a series of humorous letters they outline their problems and encourage Duncan, and all children, to be more creative and inventive in their use of colour.

2016 ***My Headteacher is a Vampire Rat!*** Written by Pamela Butchart and illustrated by Thomas Flintham (pub Nosy Crow)

A new hilarious and madcap adventure for Izzy and her friends. At school the children have a new scary headteacher, Mr Graves. Why does he look so strange and what are the unusual things in his office? As before, their imaginations run riot and they are convinced there are rats and vampires at large. They bake some garlic muffins to use as a test but events go badly wrong. You will get pulled along laughing as the real truth unravels about their new scary headteacher. Edge of your seat comedy for young and old alike enlivened hugely by the entertaining illustrations by Thomas Flintham.

2017 ***An Eagle in the Snow*** Written by Michael Morpurgo and illustrated by Michael Foreman (pub HarperCollins)

A tale entwined within a tale: the story of the most decorated private in World War One is told by a stranger to a young boy, whilst their train takes cover in a tunnel from a Messerschmitt in World War Two. The boy has to learn to confront and overcome his own fears, whilst considering the moral dilemma faced by Private Billy Byron, who thought he'd chosen to 'do the right thing' but had actually, through showing true humanity, inadvertently caused great and widespread suffering. The picture of an eagle in the snow is haunting, vivid and unsettling and remains with you long after finishing the book.

6

Branching Out

Story Aid, 25th Anniversary, National Share-a-Story Month, the Federation Gift, Carousel.

Story Aid

As part of the United Nations International Literacy Year in 1990, the Federation was involved in the Story Aid Fundraising Project, raising thousands of pounds and collecting thousands of books to go overseas. A collection of good second-hand books was packed into boxes, collected by members of the Rotary Club and sent to the Ranfurly Library who distributed them to Papua New Guinea, Guyana, Tanzania and Zambia.

The project was extended until 2000 via the Ranfurly Library, which subsequently became Book Aid International. The Isle of Wight CBG managed to collect 41 boxes of books!

The Federation has made an important contribution to the quality of children's books.

Klaus Flugge, M.D. Andersen Press

Story Aid display, 1991.

The anthology *Stories Round the World,* in partnership with Hodder and Stoughton Publishers, was developed for Story Aid. The initial long list of 57 short stories compiled from members' suggestions was sent out to the book groups and individual members to be tested. Some stories were tested by children reading on their own, others by teachers reading to their class and many by parents during family storytelling. In total the stories were tested by 21,000 children round the world.

In 1993 the Federation's Silver Jubilee Conference was held in Stratford-upon-Avon. Speakers included Bernard Ashley, Michael Morpurgo, Anne Fine, Malorie Blackman, Shirley Hughes and Terry Pratchett. It also established the proud tradition of cake at every conference.

Two boys envying the 25th birthday cake at the Stratford-upon-Avon Conference, 1993.

The Federation Gift

The Federation Gift, which was created in 1997, consists of a selection of books, and has been presented annually by the book group organising the conference, to a wide variety of charities ranging from women's refuges and children's hospices to international reading organisations.

National Share-A-Story Month

Between 1984 and 1997 the launches of National Tell-A-Story Week attracted national publicity and raised money through the sale of booklists, balloons and stickers, all linked to the annual theme. Sponsorship was obtained for every year and the events were significant in terms of outreach, involving many thousands of children and hundreds of schools, libraries and museums across the UK. There was also media interest with interviews with local TV and radio at the launch events. In 1998 NTASW became National Share-A-Story Month, namely the whole of May each year.

Examples of events in the period include telling stories:

- on the Roman Wall
- in a farmyard (York CBG)
- with the Town Crier (Blandford CBG)
- with the Laughing Policeman
- when planting a white hornbeam (Lewes CBG)

There have been jazz bands, highly coloured caravans (with husbands hiding behind the steering wheel so they couldn't be spotted!), fire-eating, African rapping and Beowulf...

Yeo Valley CBG creative efforts.

Launch of *Carousel*

1995 saw the launch of *Carousel*, a full colour review magazine. Although independent from the Federation, it was edited by David and Jenny Blanch, both Past Chairs of the Federation. Its reviews and articles, many from Federation members, still provide informative insight and expert judgement for parents, teachers and librarians. It is now the only review of children's books still in print and is a valuable resource about children's books.

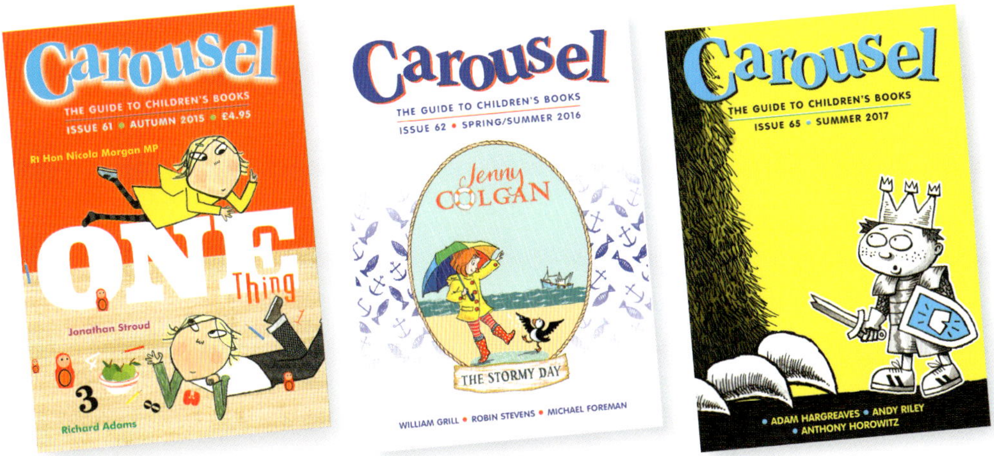

Carousel magazine covers.

The Fourth Anthology

In 1993 the Federation celebrated 25 years with the publication of '*What's For Dinner?*'. The anthology was illustrated by Mick Inkpen, with the text by Jacqui Thomas. The stories were selected by booksellers, children's book reviewers and movers and shakers in the world of children's books to raise money for the Federation.

7

Bearing Fruit

The Children's Book Award around the UK, the Federation expands its influence, the website and other resources.

The Children's Book Award and Sponsorship

The Children's Book Award was generously sponsored from 2003-2015 by The Book People and in 2018 by BookLife. As the award expanded, the location of the ceremony changed across the country, from children

Dick King-Smith, Overall Winner 1995, at the Kensington Roof Gardens.

coming face to face with flamingos at the Kensington Roof Gardens to the marquees and mud at the Hay Festival from 2006-2009. From there the ceremony moved to the Royal Botanic Gardens in Birmingham for the next 3 years until it became part of the Imagine Children's Festival in the Queen Elizabeth Hall on the Southbank in London in 2012. Its current home is the Union Jack Club in London.

Above: Rick Yancey, Overall Winner, 2014 at the Imagine Festival, London.
Left: J.K. Rowling, Overall Winner, 1999 at the Kensington Roof Gardens.

The Golden Age of Anthologies

This decade was also the golden age of anthologies, which provided parents with tried and tested stories to read with their children and also raised funds for the Federation. In 1999 *Turning Points* was a Top Ten anthology celebrating 20 years of the Children's Book Award. In 2001 *Up to the Stars* was a poetry anthology, created with Hodder who also assisted with the 2002 *Out of This World* collection. In 2005 *You Can't Bring That In Here* was created with the support of Random House Publishers.

A selection of Federation anthologies.

National Year of Reading: extending resources and joining the on-line revolution

The National Year of Reading, launched by the UK government in 1998, sought to involve everyone in a wide-ranging campaign to encourage and promote reading. Sinéad and Martin Kromer, who were Joint National Secretaries at that time, decided to attend the London launch. Sinéad Kromer completed and submitted the bid asking for £20,000, mainly to fund the setting up of new Book Groups but also to fund a fully equipped FCBG National Office. The bid was successful and the Federation received a grant of £20,000, which was used to fund the start-up of 8 new book groups and to support the 46 existing book groups.

Sinéad then worked for about 10 years with all new Book Groups, helping them get established, encouraging them to come to Conference and ensuring they got free supplies of Carousel and FCBG

Martin and Sinéad Kromer present the cheque to Seven Stories.

Newsletters for the first couple of years. Martin Kromer equipped the office, bought a phone, fax machine and a computer, established our email address, info@fcbg.org.uk, and, with the help of his son, designed the first website and established the domain name, www.fcbg.org.uk. The website has since gone from strength to strength.

The grant also funded the booklists '*Love at First Sigh*' and '*Boys Do Read!*' and it is still used to provide a start-up grant to new book groups.

Support for Seven Stories

In 2005, the Federation supported the foundation of Seven Stories, The National Centre for Children's Books in Newcastle-upon-Tyne, with a financial donation.

The work they've done over the years to bring books and children together has done immeasurable good in this country and I hope it continues for the next 50 years!

Adèle Geras, Author

Bookaroo

In 2007, Past Chair Jo Williams, who had earlier played a major role in running the Children's Book Award, became the driving force in the creation of Bookaroo, the first children's literature festival in Delhi. She and two Indian colleagues, over the last ten years, have brought thousands of children and books together in festivals all over the Indian subcontinent. Their work was acknowledged when Bookaroo won the London Book Fair International Excellence Award in 2017.

8

Harvesting Fruit

National Non-Fiction Day, two major new outreach initiatives and industry recognition of the work of the Federation.

In 2008 St Albans CBG donated 'The Armchair Traveller' to Seven Stories, comprising 495 children's books which were originally the basis of their Summer Reading Club. The project ran for over 30 years and was the forerunner of the Summer Reading Challenge. The group was keen to keep children reading through the summer holidays by travelling the world from the comfort of their armchair. To read more about this project visit https://www.sevenstories.org.uk/blog/all-about-dogs

National Non-Fiction Day

National Non-Fiction Day was created in 2010 to mark the significance of non-fiction books for the development and

Right: Chris Lloyd launching National Non-Fiction Day.

enjoyment of reading. It has expanded, like many other Federation initiatives, into National Non-Fiction November and the resources available on the website have supported activities wherever they are held. This initiative has balanced the emphasis on story and imagination with the lure of finding out about things.

Eleanor Farjeon Festival of Children's Literature

In 2011 the Federation received the Eleanor Farjeon Award and celebrated in 2013 with a Festival of Children's Literature at Birmingham Conservatoire linking storytelling with art, music and drama. Michael Morpurgo and Emma Chichester Clark discussed Pinocchio and James Mayhew, working with children in the 10-14 age range, illustrated T. H. White's *The Sword in the stone* whilst it was performed by young musicians from the Conservatoire using Benjamin Britten's music. David Almond talked of 15 years of *Skellig*, exploring its adaptation for opera, theatre and film and Clara Vulliamy hosted an exciting mini puppet toy theatre workshop. In all, over 650 children were entranced and entertained throughout the day.

Michael Morpurgo at the Children's Festival of Literature, 2013.

> The Federation of Children's Book Groups is one of a kind.
>
> *Kevin Crossley-Holland,*
> *Author, poet and translator*

The Jean Russell Storytelling Project

2016 was the year of the Jean Russell Storytelling Project, born from the Jean Russell Gift, reaching out to vulnerable and less privileged children through the power of stories. The project is in partnership with and supported by the Ragdoll Foundation and in 2016 ran throughout the year, working with young carers and reaching thousands of children in hospitals, in schools in deprived areas and at Community Arts Festivals.

Anna Conomos, international performance storyteller extraordinaire, worked with six local children's book groups across the UK, helping young people create their own stories and perform them to others. Each project was designed to leave a legacy: through enabling the children to take their own stories away with them, by using local stories across generations to create a lasting sense of community, by encouraging parents and carers to tell stories to their children and by helping children become storytellers themselves to the children who follow them. A new project with the same focus on 'Story Cooking' took place during 2018.

Left: Anna Conomos with children from Oxford CBG, 2016.

Afterword

The Story Continues

"The Federation led the way in children's books. It was the first to do things that are now normal. It was started by people who knew very little, were not experienced and found they could do things they never thought they could do – and they could! Stories is the key word." Pat Thomson.

Stories are a catalyst for the imagination, releasing children's creativity and books are often the starting point for a magical epiphany. The Federation leads the way in bringing books and children together in families, in schools and in libraries.

The strength of the Federation has always lain in its community-based groups. In this modern world, in which we are all so connected and yet also so isolated, this is key. And in a time in which local libraries are closing and school library budgets have been slashed, and yet reading for pleasure has been recognised as being fundamental to building empathy and understanding others, the Federation has never been more relevant.

The children's book groups began with interested parents and, while some groups remain parent focused, many have widened their circle to include, for example, schools, libraries, hospitals and young carers. Individual members and professional members also support national initiatives and enjoy catching up with each other at Conference.

The Federation is not resting on its laurels and is embracing new technology to keep everyone updated. The use of Twitter, blogging and Facebook has offered new opportunities to bring children and books together.

Our next 50 years will no doubt see other challenges, with the continuing need to recruit volunteers, maintain effective fund-raising and sponsorship and keep up-to-date with the changing nature of book groups.

Wherever they come from, Federation members will remain passionate about children's books. Their commitment to the Federation's mission to bring children and books together, will maintain the Federation's focus on the power of story to foster creative imagination and to give children a voice.

We do not know what the future will bring, but we do know that whatever happens the members of the Federation will be there fighting for the right of the child to have free access to books, ensuring that all the good work of the past 50 years continues.

Appendix A

List of Anthologies

All the stories included in each anthology were tested by members of the groups. This testing, whether stories were read aloud by adults to groups or shared in the family, confirmed the importance of the children's voices in the selection process, thereby boosting their critical reasoning and confidence.

1976: *Stories for Children* chosen by parents for reading aloud, edited by Anne Wood, published by Hodder.

1986: *Our Best Stories*, edited by Anne Wood and Ann Pilling, published by Hodder.

1990: *Stories Round the World,* foreword by Thelma Simpson, published by Hodder for Story Aid, using stories tested by 21,000 children round the world.

1993: *What's for Dinner?* published by Hodder – an anthology of favourite stories to celebrate 25 years of the FCBG.

1996: *Simply the Best* illustrated by Anthony Lewis, foreword by Pat Triggs published by Hodder to celebrate 20 years of NTASW.

1999: *Turning Points:* Top Ten anthology celebrating 20 years of the Children's Book Award.

2001: *Up to the Stars,* illustrated by Alan Marks, this poetry anthology was published by Hodder, tested by children and schools.

2002: *Out of This World* published by Hodder.

2005: *You Can't Bring That in Here* foreword by Pat Thomson, published by Random House, was a collection of funny stories.

Appendix B

List of Booklists

There is no comprehensive archive of all the age and genre related booklists including Pick of the Year Lists as yet. Annual booklists were also produced for NSSM. The titles below are the most recent booklists.

- It's Never Too Early To Start!
- Going Solo
- Up and Running
- If you like this
- It's A Fact
- Teen and Beyond
- Inside the box
- More Poetry Please
- Kick Off
- Picture Books for Older Children
- Books to Enjoy with Under-Fives
- Starting a Home Library
- Explore the World of Children's Books
- Share A Story
- Annual booklists linked to NSSM 1984 to late 1990s
- Love at First Sigh!
- Boys Do Read

The Federation of Children's Book Groups
"GOING SOLO"
A selection of books especially chosen for the newly independent reader
The Federation of Children's Book Groups
"Up and Running"
THE FEDERATION OF CHILDREN'S BOOK GROUPS
INSIDE THE BOX
A SELECTION OF COMICS AND GRAPHIC NOVELS FOR ALL AGES
IF YOU LIKE THIS... THEN WHY NOT TRY THIS?
A booklist of fabulous recommended reading for children aged 8-12 years
Compiled by Herts Children's Book Group for the Federation of Children's Book Groups, Spring 2014.

Book lists.

Appendix C

The Children's Book Award Winners

1981 *Mr Magnolia* Quentin Blake
1982 *Fair's Fair* Leon Garfield & Margaret Chamberlain
1983 *The BFG* Roald Dahl & Quentin Blake
1984 *Erik the Viking* Terry Jones & Michael Foreman
1985 *Brother in the Land* Robert Swindells
1986 *What About Arthur?* Amanda Graham & Donna Erynell
1987 *The Jolly Postman* Allan and Janet Ahlberg
1988 *Winnie the Witch* Valerie Thomas & Korky Paul
1989 *Matilda* Roald Dahl & Quentin Blake
1990 *Room 13* Robert Swindells
1991 *Threadbear* Mick Inkpen
1992 *Kiss the Dust* Elizabeth Laird
1993 *The Suitcase Kid* Jacqueline Wilson
1994 *The Boy in the Bubble* Ian Strachan
1995 *Harriet's Hare* Dick King Smith
1996 *Double Act* Jacqueline Wilson
1997 *The Hundred-Mile-an-Hour Dog* Jeremy Strong
1998 *Harry Potter and the Philosopher's Stone* J.K. Rowling
1999 *Harry Potter and the Chamber of Secrets* J.K. Rowling
2000 *Kensuke's Kingdom* Michael Morpurgo & Michael Foreman
2001 *Eat Your Peas* Nick Sharratt
2002 *Noughts and Crosses* Malorie Blackman
2003 *Skeleton Key* Anthony Horowitz
2004 *Private Peaceful* Michael Morpurgo
2005 *Baby Brains* Simon James

2006 *Percy Jackson and the Lightning Thief* Rick Riordan
2007 *You're a Bad Man, Mr Gum!* Andy Stanton
2008 *Skulduggery Pleasant* Derek Landy
2009 *Blood Ties* Sophie McKenzie
2010 *The Hunger Games* Suzanne Collins
2011 *Shadow* Michael Morpurgo & Christian Birmingham
2012 *A Monster Calls* Patrick Ness
2013 *The Spooky Spooky House* Andrew Weale & Lee Wildish
2014 *The Fifth Wave* Rick Yancey
2015 *The Day the Crayons Quit* Oliver Jeffers & Drew Daywalt
2016 *My Head Teacher Is a Vampire Rat!* Pamela Butchart & Thomas Flintham
2017 *An Eagle in the Snow* by Michael Morpurgo & Michael Foreman.

Index